HERE'S WHERE HISTORY HAPPENED!

THE WHITE HOUSE

BY JANEY LEVY

Gareth Stevens
PUBLISHING

Please visit our website, www.garethstevens.com. For a free color catalog of all our high-quality books, call toll free 1-800-542-2595 or fax 1-877-542-2596.

Library of Congress Cataloging-in-Publication Data
Names: Levy, Janey, author.
Title: The White House / Janey Levy.
Description: [Buffalo, New York] : Gareth Stevens Publishing, [2025] | Series: Here's where history happened! | Includes bibliographical references and index. | Audience: Grades 2-3
Identifiers: LCCN 2023054179 (print) | LCCN 2023054180 (ebook) | ISBN 9781482466478 (library binding) | ISBN 9781482466461 (paperback) | ISBN 9781482466485 (ebook)
Subjects: LCSH: White House (Washington, D.C.)–Juvenile literature. | Washington (D.C.)–Buildings, structures, etc.–Juvenile literature. | Presidents–United States–Juvenile literature.
Classification: LCC F204.W5 L57 2025 (print) | LCC F204.W5 (ebook) | DDC 725/.1709753–dc23/eng/20231205
LC record available at https://lccn.loc.gov/2023054179
LC ebook record available at https://lccn.loc.gov/2023054180

Published in 2025 by
Gareth Stevens Publishing
2544 Clinton Street
Buffalo, NY 14224

Designer: Tanya Dellaccio Keeney
Editor: Theresa Emminizer

Photo credits: Series background pixelparticle/Shutterstock.com; cover David Evison/Shutterstock.com; p. 5 (top) Zack Frank/Shutterstock.com; p. 5 (bottom) lazyllama/Shutterstock.com; p. 7 (Washington) ra3rn/Shutterstock.com; p. 7 (map) Maps Expert/Shutterstock.com; pp. 9, 15 Courtesy of the Library of Congress; p. 11 (top) https://upload.wikimedia.org/wikipedia/commons/f/f6/Hoban_-_White_House_Design.jpg; p. 11 (bottom) https://upload.wikimedia.org/wikipedia/commons/4/40/Pierre_Charles_L%27Enfant.jpg; p. 13 (top left) Damien Storan/Shutterstock.com; p. 13 (top right) vichie81/Shutterstock.com; p. 13 (bottom left) Lucky-photographer/Shutterstock.com; p. 13 (bottom right) https://upload.wikimedia.org/wikipedia/commons/2/23/Château_de_Rastignac.JPG; p. 17 (top) https://upload.wikimedia.org/wikipedia/commons/f/f2/Burning_of_Washington_1814.jpg; p. 17 (bottom) https://upload.wikimedia.org/wikipedia/commons/8/8b/Dolley_Madison.jpg; p. 19 https://upload.wikimedia.org/wikipedia/commons/c/c7/Obama_edits_speech_before_announcing_death_of_Osama_bin_Laden.jpg.

Printed in the United States of America

CPSIA compliance information: Batch #CSGS25: For further information contact Gareth Stevens at 1-800-542-2595.

CONTENTS

Words in the glossary appear in **bold** type the first time they are used in the text.

WELCOME TO THE WHITE HOUSE!

You've likely heard of the White House. It's where the U.S. president lives and works. Yes, that's right—the president lives *and* works there. There are separate spaces for living and working.

The White House is located in the national capital, Washington, DC. Did you know the country's early leaders decided to build the White House as a special home for the president? And did you know Washington, DC, itself had to be created? This book tells the story of both!

THESE PICTURES SHOW BOTH SIDES OF THE WHITE HOUSE. THE SOUTH SIDE, SHOWN IN THE BOTTOM PICTURE, IS THE SIDE MOST OFTEN SHOWN IN PICTURES.

KNOW THE FACTS!

GEORGE WASHINGTON NEVER LIVED IN THE WHITE HOUSE. IT HADN'T BEEN COMPLETED YET WHILE HE WAS PRESIDENT! JOHN ADAMS WAS THE FIRST PRESIDENT TO LIVE THERE.

WHERE TO PUT THE NATION'S NEW CAPITAL?

Choosing a spot for the new capital required a **compromise**. Northern leaders wanted it in the North. Southern leaders wanted it in the South. It wound up in the South. But to make northern leaders happy, the new national government agreed to pay the states' **debts** from the **American Revolution**.

President George Washington chose a spot on the north side of the Potomac River for the new capital. Maryland and Virginia gave up some of their land for it.

THIS MAP SHOWS THE LOCATION OF WASHINGTON, DC, WHERE THE WHITE HOUSE IS FOUND.

KNOW THE FACTS!

HOW WAS THE NEW CAPITAL NAMED? THE AREA WAS NAMED THE DISTRICT OF COLUMBIA IN HONOR OF CHRISTOPHER COLUMBUS. THE CITY WAS NAMED WASHINGTON IN HONOR OF GEORGE WASHINGTON.

CREATING THE NEW CAPITAL

How do you create a new capital? You hire someone who plans cities! In 1791, Washington hired a man from France named Pierre L'Enfant (pea-EHR lawn-FAWNT).

Thomas Jefferson gave L'Enfant maps of European cities to use as models. L'Enfant took ideas from several of them. His city plan included long, grand streets laid out in a **grid**. Other broad streets cut across the grid in diagonal, or sloping, lines. The plan centered on the president's house and the Capitol, where Congress would meet.

KNOW THE FACTS!

L'ENFANT HAD BEEN IN THE UNITED STATES A LONG TIME. HE CAME IN 1776 TO HELP THE COLONISTS FIGHT IN THE AMERICAN REVOLUTION.

THIS MAP, MADE IN 1792, SHOWS WHAT L'ENFANT'S PLAN FOR WASHINGTON, DC, LOOKED LIKE.

CREATING THE PRESIDENT'S HOUSE

Besides planning the new capital city, the nation's leaders had to decide what sort of house the president should have. L'Enfant created a **design** for one. It was a huge, grand palace five times the size of the present-day White House!

But L'Enfant was fired because he was hard to work with. So a **contest** was held to find a new design for the president's house. Nine designs were presented. Washington chose the design by an Irish **architect**, James Hoban.

KNOW THE FACTS!

THE WHITE HOUSE WAS ORIGINALLY CALLED THE PRESIDENT'S HOUSE, THE PRESIDENT'S PALACE, OR THE EXECUTIVE MANSION. PRESIDENT THEODORE ROOSEVELT OFFICIALLY NAMED IT THE WHITE HOUSE IN 1901.

THIS GIVES AN IDEA OF WHAT PIERRE L'ENFANT LOOKED LIKE. "PIERRE" IS THE FRENCH FORM OF THE NAME "PETER," AND HE WENT BY PETER IN THE UNITED STATES.

JAMES HOBAN AND HIS DESIGN

James Hoban was born in Ireland around 1760 and studied at the Dublin Society School of Architectural Drawing in Dublin, Ireland. He came to the United States around 1785.

You might be surprised to discover that Hoban modeled his design on buildings he knew in Ireland. His design looks much like certain Irish country houses, which were homes of wealthy people. Compare the pictures on the next page to see how much the White House looks like some Irish buildings!

DO THE IRISH BUILDINGS ON THE RIGHT LOOK LIKE THE WHITE HOUSE?

KNOW THE FACTS!

IT WAS WASHINGTON HIMSELF WHO SUGGESTED HOBAN ENTER THE CONTEST TO DESIGN THE WHITE HOUSE.

BUILDING THE WHITE HOUSE

Construction of the White House began on October 13, 1792. It was built of sandstone that came from 40 miles (64 km) away. It took eight years to build the White House and cost $232,372. That's equal to about $100 million today!

Finding workers to build the White House was hard. The young country didn't have many skilled carpenters and stone workers. So workers had to be brought over from Europe. Many enslaved and free African Americans also worked hard to build the White House.

KNOW THE FACTS!

MORE WORK WAS DONE ON THE WHITE HOUSE UNDER PRESIDENT THOMAS JEFFERSON. ARCHITECT BENJAMIN LATROBE FIXED THE LEAKING ROOF, PUT IN A GRAND STAIRCASE, AND EVEN PUT IN TOILETS!

THIS IS AN EARLY PICTURE OF THE WHITE HOUSE. IT WAS COATED WITH WHITE PAINT TO PROTECT THE SANDSTONE IN 1798.

THE WHITE HOUSE BURNS!

From 1812 to 1815, the United States fought another war with England, called the War of 1812. In August 1814, the British captured Washington, DC, and burned down the city—including the White House! The inside of the White House was destroyed.

For a while, Congress actually considered moving the capital to Cincinnati, Ohio! In the end, though, they decided to rebuild. James Hoban was even brought back to rebuild the White House. He finished his work in 1817.

THIS SHOWS AN ARTIST'S IDEA OF WHAT THE BURNING OF THE WHITE HOUSE LOOKED LIKE.

KNOW THE FACTS!

DOLLEY MADISON, WIFE OF PRESIDENT JAMES MADISON, SAVED A PAINTING OF GEORGE WASHINGTON AND A COPY OF THE **DECLARATION OF INDEPENDENCE**. SHE TOOK THESE WITH HER AS SHE ESCAPED THE CITY.

CHANGES THROUGH THE YEARS

Many changes have been made to the White House over the years. President Theodore Roosevelt (1901–1909) added the West Wing for the president's offices. President Howard Taft created the famous Oval Office in 1909.

In 1927, the third-floor **attic** was changed into a living area. The East Wing, for the First Lady's offices, was finished in 1946. While Harry Truman was president (1945–1953), it was discovered that the White House was about to fall down. It had to be almost completely rebuilt!

KNOW THE FACTS!

THERE WAS A FIRE IN THE WEST WING IN 1929, WHILE HERBERT HOOVER WAS PRESIDENT.

THIS IS THE OVAL OFFICE, THE PRESIDENT'S OFFICE. IT LOOKS DIFFERENT UNDER DIFFERENT PRESIDENTS BECAUSE PRESIDENTS CHANGE THE FURNITURE, RUGS, AND CURTAINS.

THE WHITE HOUSE TODAY

Today visitors can tour the White House. But visitors must plan in advance. Visitors must request, or ask for, a tour through their member of Congress. Visitors from other countries must contact their **embassy** in Washington, DC, to request a tour. Requests must be made at least three weeks in advance and no more than three months in advance.

About half a million people visit the White House each year. Maybe one day you'll be one of them!

KNOW THE FACTS!

TOURS ARE FREE AND TAKE PLACE ON TUESDAY, WEDNESDAY, THURSDAY, FRIDAY, AND SATURDAY.

FANTASTIC FACTS ABOUT THE WHITE HOUSE

SIX LEVELS

55,000 SQUARE FEET (5109.6 SQ M)

132 ROOMS

35 BATHROOMS

412 DOORS

147 WINDOWS

28 FIREPLACES

8 STAIRCASES

3 ELEVATORS

570 GALLONS OF PAINT TO COVER THE OUTSIDE

KITCHEN CAN MAKE FOOD FOR 140 PEOPLE

THESE ARE SOME OF THE AMAZING FACTS ABOUT THE BUILDING WHERE THE PRESIDENT LIVES AND WORKS.

GLOSSARY

American Revolution: The war in which the colonies won their freedom from England.

architect: A person who designs buildings.

attic: A space just below the roof of a building that's often used to store objects.

compromise: A way of two sides reaching agreement in which each gives up something to end an argument.

contest: An event in which people try to win by doing something better than others in the event.

debt: An amount of money owed.

Declaration of Independence: The piece of writing in which the colonies said they were free from British rule.

design: The pattern or shape of something. Also, to create the pattern or shape of something.

embassy: The people who represent their country in another country. Also, the building where these people work.

grid: A set of squares formed by crisscrossing lines.

FOR MORE INFORMATION

Books

Lewis, Cicely. *The Real History of the White House*. Minneapolis, MN: Lerner Publications, 2023.

Ward, Lindsay. *The White House: A Meet the Nation's Capital Book*. New York, NY: Harper, 2024.

Websites

About the White House
www.whitehouse.gov/about-the-white-house/

Read about the White House and past presidents on the official website.

White House Facts for Kids
https://kids.kiddle.co/White_House
Discover more about the White House here, and see lots of pictures.

Publisher's note to educators and parents: Our editors have carefully reviewed these websites to ensure that they are suitable for students. Many websites change frequently, however, and we cannot guarantee that a site's future contents will continue to meet our high standards of quality and educational value. Be advised that students should be closely supervised whenever they access the internet.

INDEX